Harry Potter™

HOUSES OF
HOGWARTS™

CINEMATIC GUIDE

SCHOLASTIC LTD.

www.harrypotter.com

Scholastic Children's Books
Euston House, 24 Eversholt Street,
London NW1 1DB, UK

A division of Scholastic Ltd
London ~ New York ~ Toronto ~ Sydney ~ Auckland
Mexico City ~ New Delhi ~ Hong Kong

First published in the US by Scholastic Inc, 2017
Published in the UK by Scholastic Ltd, 2017

By Felicity Baker
Art Direction: Rick DeMonico
Page Design: Heather Barber

ISBN 978 1407 17319 1

Printed in the UK by Bell and Bain Ltd, Glasgow

2 4 6 8 10 9 7 5 3 1

Papers used by Scholastic Children's Books are
made from wood grown in sustainable forests.

www.scholastic.co.uk

Contents

Introduction

At Hogwarts School of
Witchcraft and Wizardry,
first-year students are sorted
into one of four houses:
Gryffindor, Ravenclaw,
Hufflepuff and Slytherin.

The Sorting Ceremony is the first event at the start of each school year. First-year students anxiously await their turn to try on the Sorting Hat and find out which house they will join.

Sometimes the Sorting Hat takes its time to decide which house is the best fit for each student. When sorting Harry Potter, the hat first thinks he would do well in Slytherin – but after Harry says he would rather be sorted into *any* house but Slytherin, it ultimately places him in Gryffindor.

Other times, the Sorting Hat knows which house a student is destined for right away. Draco Malfoy was sorted into Slytherin before the hat was even placed all the way on to his head!

The House Cup competition takes place throughout the course of the school year. Students are awarded points for their houses when they do something well and lose points if they break any rules.

Hermione Granger often wins points for Gryffindor for her impressive spell casting during lessons.

Some teachers, like Professor Snape and Professor Umbridge, seem to show favouritism when awarding or taking away house points.

At the end of the year, Professor Dumbledore announces the house that has the most points and awards it the honour of the House Cup.

Gryffindor

Gryffindor house is home to those who are courageous, determined and chivalrous. Gryffindor students often dive head first into new adventures. The house colours are red and gold and the house crest features a lion as a symbol of bravery.

The Gryffindor common room is located in one of the towers of Hogwarts castle.

To enter Gryffindor Tower, a student must give the correct password to the painting that guards the entrance, which students refer to as 'the Fat Lady'.

Fred and George Weasley often enlist younger students in the common room to test out their latest joke inventions.

Gryffindor students frequently gather to celebrate in the common room, especially when their team wins an important Quidditch match.

One of the Gryffindor boys' dormitories is home to Harry Potter and his friends Ron Weasley, Neville Longbottom, Dean Thomas and Seamus Finnigan.

Professor McGonagall is Head of Gryffindor house. Though she is strict, she is also fair and kind-hearted.

"The house of Godric Gryffindor has commanded the respect of the wizarding world for nearly ten centuries. I will not have you, in the course of a single evening besmirching that name by behaving like a babbling, bumbling band of baboons!"

—PROFESSOR MCGONAGALL, *HARRY POTTER AND THE GOBLET OF FIRE* FILM

Professor McGonagall does not hesitate to take points from her own house if a Gryffindor breaks the rules – something Harry, Ron and Hermione learn the hard way when they are caught sneaking out after hours.

Though she is impartial when awarding house points, Professor McGonagall loves to cheer on the Gryffindor Quidditch team.

Harry, Hermione and Ron are true Gryffindors; their daring and bravery often lead them on wild adventures – and into dangerous situations.

In their first year, Harry, Ron and Hermione battle their way through a series of enchantments to reach the Philosopher's Stone before it is stolen by a Dark wizard.

In their second year, the three friends secretly brew Polyjuice Potion in the girls' bathroom.

In their third year, the trio comes face-to-face with a werewolf
– who also happens to be their usually mild-mannered Defence
Against the Dark Arts teacher, Professor Lupin.

All six of Ron's siblings are proud Gryffindors as well. The Weasleys each bring their own unique strengths to Gryffindor house.

"Ha! Another Weasley. I know just what to do with you ... Gryffindor!"

—THE SORTING HAT TO RON WEASLEY, *HARRY POTTER AND THE PHILOSOPHER'S STONE* FILM

Percy Weasley is a Gryffindor prefect, a title given to a select few older students in each house. Prefects are responsible for guiding first-years, setting an example for all of their classmates and – perhaps Percy's favourite – maintaining order by enforcing rules.

Fred and George Weasley are twins and notorious pranksters.

Ginny Weasley is known for casting powerful jinxes. She plays Chaser on the Gryffindor Quidditch team.

The timid Neville Longbottom does not immediately show the typical qualities found in a Gryffindor. However, it isn't long before he proves that he is a true Gryffindor.

Everyone is proud of Neville when he finally perfects the Disarming Spell during a meeting of Dumbledore's Army, a secret student group formed to combat Dark magic.

In his seventh year, Neville fearlessly stands up to a group of Death Eaters who come aboard the Hogwarts Express in search of Harry Potter.

"*It takes a great deal of bravery to stand up to your enemies, but a great deal more to stand up to your friends. I award ten points to Neville Longbottom.*"

—PROFESSOR DUMBLEDORE, *HARRY POTTER AND THE PHILOSOPHER'S STONE* FILM

During the final battle against Voldemort at Hogwarts, Neville destroys Voldemort's last Horcrux: one of seven pieces of Voldemort's soul hidden inside precious objects to help him live for ever. In this case, the Horcrux was contained inside the Dark Lord's pet snake, Nagini.

The Gryffindors are passionate about their Quidditch team! Harry earns the coveted role of Seeker in his first year and he joins a team of talented players.

When Harry first joins the Gryffindor Quidditch team he meets Oliver Wood, the team's captain. Oliver is a Keeper and he takes winning very seriously.

Lee Jordan is the Quidditch match commentator. Over the stadium loudspeaker, he shares his knowledge and love of the game with a crowd of roaring fans.

The Gryffindor section of the Quidditch stadium is always packed with cheering students sporting their house colours.

The Sword of Gryffindor was once owned by Godric Gryffindor, the founder of the house. It plays a crucial role in many of the Gryffindor students' bravest moments.

While in the Chamber of Secrets, Harry pulls the Sword of Gryffindor out of the Sorting Hat and uses it to battle a Basilisk.

"It would take a true Gryffindor to pull that out of the hat."

—Professor Dumbledore, *Harry Potter and the Chamber of Secrets* film

Years later, the sword mysteriously appears at the bottom of a frozen lake.

Harry dives in to retrieve it, nearly drowning.

Ron rescues Harry, then uses the sword to destroy Salazar Slytherin's locket, a Horcrux.

Ravenclaw

Rowena Ravenclaw founded Ravenclaw house for students who value learning, wisdom, intelligence and wit. Ravenclaws have sharp minds and take great pride in their studies. Their house colours are blue and bronze and the house symbol is an eagle.

The Head of Ravenclaw house is Professor Flitwick. He is a cheerful, good-natured wizard who teaches Charms.

Professor Flitwick often addresses his class while standing on a tower of books so he can see everyone better.

In Harry, Ron and Hermione's first Charms lesson, Professor Flitwick teaches the Levitation Charm, *Wingardium Leviosa*. The professor is impressed when Hermione masters the spell right away.

Every year during the holidays, Professor Flitwick uses his expert Charms skills to help decorate Hogwarts castle.

Though she is sometimes teased by her classmates, quirky Ravenclaw Luna Lovegood always has words of wisdom to share with her friends and classmates.

Like Harry, Luna is able to see Thestrals, magical beasts who only appear to those who have witnessed death.

Harry: "What are they?"

Luna: "They're called Thestrals. They're quite gentle, really, but people avoid them because they're a bit..."

Harry: "Different."

—HARRY POTTER AND THE ORDER OF THE PHOENIX FILM

Luna comforts Harry as he mourns the death of his godfather, Sirius Black.

"*Anyway, my mum always said things we lose have a way of coming back to us in the end. If not always in the way we expect.*"

—LUNA LOVEGOOD, *HARRY POTTER AND THE ORDER OF THE PHOENIX* FILM

Luna becomes friends with Harry, Ron and Hermione in their fifth year. She often accompanies them on their risky schemes and adventures.

Luna learns to produce a Patronus Charm at a meeting of Dumbledore's Army, the secret student defence group.

When Harry needs to find a way to get to the Department of Mysteries to help Sirius, Luna comes to the rescue. She suggests they fly there on Thestrals!

Neville and Luna share a peaceful moment after fighting in the Battle of Hogwarts.

Cho Chang is another Ravenclaw student who befriends many members of other houses.

Cho Chang attends the Yule Ball with Hufflepuff student Cedric Diggory.

Cho is a member of Dumbledore's Army along with many Gryffindors, Hufflepuffs and fellow Ravenclaws.

"You're a really good teacher, Harry. I've never been able to Stun anything before."

—CHO CHANG, HARRY POTTER AND THE ORDER OF THE PHOENIX FILM

Harry and Cho share a kiss.

Hogwarts founder, Rowena Ravenclaw, had a precious jewelled crown, known as a diadem. It was lost for centuries until Voldemort found it and turned it into a Horcrux.

Cho Chang and Luna Lovegood tell Harry about the lost diadem. Luna knows exactly how they can find the missing Horcrux.

Luna seeks out the ghost of Ravenclaw Tower, the Grey Lady – whose real name is Helena Ravenclaw. She is Rowena Ravenclaw's daughter.

> "It's here, in the castle. In the place where everything is hidden. If you have to ask, you'll never know. If you know, you need only ask."
>
> —Helena Ravenclaw, *Harry Potter and the Deathly Hallows – Part 2* film

Harry follows the Grey Lady's riddle and locates the diadem in the Room of Requirement. Now he can destroy this Horcrux once and for all.

Hufflepuff

Helga Hufflepuff was very open-minded about who she would accept into her house. As a result, Hufflepuffs exemplify many admirable qualities, such as loyalty, fairness, kindness and tolerance. Their house animal is a badger and their colours are black and yellow.

The Head of Hufflepuff House is Professor Sprout, a friendly witch who teaches Herbology.

Hogwarts students learn about all kinds of magical flowers and plants in their Herbology lessons.

Professor Sprout teaches her students about Mandrakes – magical plants that look like babies and have a cry that can be fatal to humans.

Professor Sprout's Herbology skills come in handy when students are Petrified – turned to stone – by a mysterious monster in the Chamber of Secrets. She prepares a special drink, called a Mandrake Draught, to return the Petrified students to full health.

Popular and well-loved, Cedric Diggory brings glory to Hufflepuff house when he is chosen to be Hogwarts champion in the Triwizard Tournament.

As the champion from Hogwarts School of Witchcraft and Wizardry, Cedric will compete against students from the wizarding schools Beauxbatons Academy of Magic and the Durmstrang Institute during a series of challenges known as 'tasks'.

Cedric shakes hands with Professor Dumbledore after the Goblet of Fire selects the Hufflepuff as Hogwarts champion.

Surprisingly, Harry is also chosen to be a Triwizard Tournament champion for Hogwarts. This mysterious selection causes many Hufflepuffs – and even Gryffindors – to question Harry's motives. In the end, Harry and Cedric help each other throughout the tournament.

After Harry warns Cedric about the dragons in the first task, Cedric returns the favour by giving Harry a clue for the second task.

Like a true Hufflepuff, Cedric competes with honesty and fairness – which makes it even harder for his classmates to accept the tragic outcome of the tournament.

During the third and final task, Harry risks losing the tournament when he stops to help Cedric escape deadly vines that ensnared him.

At the end of the competition, Cedric and Harry fall into a trap and come face-to-face with Lord Voldemort in a dark graveyard. Harry fights bravely and manages to narrowly escape, but not before Cedric is killed by Peter Pettigrew at Voldemort's command.

Cedric's classmates mourn his untimely death – a tragedy that soon becomes a major turning point for the wizarding world: Lord Voldemort is back.

"Cedric Diggory was, as you all know, exceptionally hard-working, infinitely fair-minded and most importantly, a fierce, fierce friend... You remember that, and we'll celebrate a boy who was kind, and honest, and brave and true. Right to the very end."

—Professor Dumbledore, *Harry Potter and the Goblet of Fire* film

Helga Hufflepuff's cup becomes one of Lord Voldemort's seven Horcruxes. The cup is hidden in Bellatrix Lestrange's Gringotts vault.

Harry, Ron and Hermione plot to get inside Bellatrix's vault. Their plan hinges on Hermione using Polyjuice Potion to disguise herself as Bellatrix.

Helga Hufflepuff's cup

Harry, Ron and Hermione do the unthinkable and successfully break into Bellatrix's vault – but they must use their wits to battle a curse she has placed on her belongings causing them to multiply!

Ron and Hermione destroy the Horcrux inside the cup using a Basilisk fang from the Chamber of Secrets.

Slytherin

Slytherin house was founded by Salazar Slytherin, the only Hogwarts founder who clashed with the other three. Slytherin values resourcefulness, ambition and cunning. Over the years, many Dark witches and wizards were sorted into Slytherin. The house colours are green and silver and the symbol is a serpent.

The Slytherin common room is located in the dungeons of Hogwarts castle.

Only Slytherin students can enter the common room and they must know the password.

In Harry and Ron's second year, they drink Polyjuice Potion to pose as Slytherin students, Vincent Crabbe and Gregory Goyle. Once transformed, they sneak into the Slytherin common room and try to trick Draco into giving them information.

When their Polyjuice Potion begins to wear off, Harry and Ron must run away before they're discovered trespassing!

For many years, Professor Snape is the head of Slytherin house.

Professor Snape teaches Potions and often shows favouritism to Slytherin students during his lessons.

After Snape becomes Headmaster of Hogwarts, Professor Slughorn steps in as Head of Slytherin house.

Professor Slughorn invites the students in his exclusive 'Slug Club' to his Christmas party. Tom Riddle, who later becomes the Dark Lord, Voldemort, was also a member of the club during his time at Hogwarts.

Many Slytherins place a high importance on being 'pure-blood', which means coming from a family that has no Muggle ancestry.

Slytherin student Draco Malfoy shares Salazar Slytherin's prejudice that pure-blood witches and wizards are superior to half-bloods or Muggle-borns.

> "Salazar Slytherin wished to be more selective about the students admitted to Hogwarts. He believed magical learning should be kept within all-magic families."
>
> —Professor McGonagall, *Harry Potter and the Chamber of Secrets* film

Draco's parents were in Slytherin house, as was his Aunt Bellatrix. They all become Death Eaters and members of Lord Voldemort's inner circle.

Draco and his fellow Slytherins often cause trouble for the other students at Hogwarts.

Draco with his friends Crabbe, Goyle and Pansy Parkinson

Draco, Crabbe and Goyle make fun of Harry after he faints during a Dementor encounter in their third year.

In their fifth year, many Slytherins join Professor Umbridge's Inquisitorial Squad: a group of students who help enforce her strict and unfair rules.

The Inquisitorial Squad does Professor Umbridge's dirty work at Hogwarts, spying on students they think are up to something, like Dumbledore's Army.

The Slytherin Quidditch team is very competitive and they don't always play by the rules.

Draco Malfoy plays Seeker for the Slytherin team.

Draco with the Slytherin Quidditch captain, Marcus Flint (left)

Slytherin plays matches against every team but their fiercest rival is always Gryffindor. Draco often taunts Harry during matches in an attempt to distract him from finding the Golden Snitch.

"Training for the ballet, Potter?"

—DRACO MALFOY, *HARRY POTTER AND THE CHAMBER OF SECRETS* FILM

The most notorious member of Slytherin house is Tom Riddle – also known as Lord Voldemort. He attended Hogwarts about fifty years before Harry and his friends were students.

As the Heir of Slytherin, Tom Riddle opens the Chamber of Secrets twice to unleash the Basilisk on Muggle-borns: once while he was a student and again years later while Harry is a student.

"*Let's match the power of Lord Voldemort, Heir of Salazar Slytherin, against the famous Harry Potter.*"

—LORD VOLDEMORT, *HARRY POTTER AND THE CHAMBER OF SECRETS* FILM

Voldemort made Salazar Slytherin's locket into one of his Horcruxes – and it was a fellow Slytherin, Regulus Black, who first attempted to thwart Voldemort's plan for immortality by stealing the locket.

Regulus Black, the brother of Harry's godfather, Sirius Black, was a Slytherin. He was the first to retrieve the locket from Voldemort's hiding place, proving that not all Slytherins are on the side of darkness.

"To the Dark Lord,
I know I will be dead long before you read this, but I want you to know that it was I who discovered your secret. I have stolen the real Horcrux and intend to destroy it as soon as I can. I face death in the hope that when you meet your match, you will be mortal once more. R.A.B."

—REGULUS BLACK, *HARRY POTTER AND THE HALF-BLOOD PRINCE* FILM

The locket ends up in the hands of Dolores Umbridge. Harry, Ron and Hermione break into the Ministry of Magic, where Umbridge is an employee, to steal the locket from her.

Ron Weasley holding the Horcrux locket after he destroyed it with the Sword of Gryffindor.

"It is not our abilities that show us what we truly are. It is our choices."

—PROFESSOR DUMBLEDORE, *HARRY POTTER AND THE CHAMBER OF SECRETS* FILM